Who Cares What You Have To Say? Your Kids!

Who Cares What You Have To Say? Your Kids!

Scriptures to pray/confess
over your children.

The tongue has the power of life and death...
(Prov 18:21)

IGIOREU OKPETU

XULON PRESS

Xulon Press
2301 Lucien Way #415
Maitland, FL 32751
407.339.4217
www.xulonpress.com

Printed in the United States of America.

ISBN-13: 978-1-6628-0091-7
Hardcover ISBN-13: 978-1-6628-0092-4
Ebook ISBN-13: 978-1-6628-0093-1

To papa and mama.

TABLE OF CONTENTS

INTRODUCTION

WHO CARES WHAT YOU HAVE TO SAY? YOUR
kids <u>do</u>. Name calling and denigrating lan-
guage is one that is generally not recom-
mended by health professionals as this
could cause permeating pain that may last
even up to adulthood. Our words as parents and guardians could prompt our loved
ones to greater heights or be the reason for a
lack of self-esteem in relationships, marriage,
school, work, parenting and even-grand
parenting. According to Dr Karen Stevens
(easternflorida.edu) "Children take words to
heart, especially those from the adults they
love. Children want and need to believe

what their parents say about them. **It's our responsibility to give them something worth believing"** It's not just what you say while they are listening, what are you saying about them even when they are not. Your child will behave according to what name you call him or her. And out of the ground the LORD God formed every beast of the field and every bird of the air, and He brought them to the man to see what he would name each one. And whatever the man called each living creature, that was its name (Gen 2:19). So what are you 'calling' or 'confessing about' your kids? The word 'confession' originates from the greek word homologeo, the first part of the word 'homou' ("together with") and 'lego' ("say") to say together with God what he says about something. In the scriptures we are admonished to speak God's word over our circumstances to align whatever we are saying to what his word says. Speaking God's word has tremendous power to turn our circumstances or situation around. This book of the law shall not depart from your mouth (Joshua 1:8) because as you decree a thing so shall it be established (Job 22:28). God's word will not return void but will accomplish the purpose for which it is being sent (Isaiah 55:11). As you speak his word to your various situations by your confessions, the one who is not a man will meet you exactly at the point of your need. You will experience God's glory as you speak life, health and faith over your loved ones.

Chapter One

HAVE FAITH IN YOUR KIDS

"Children are likely to live up to what you believe of them." — Lady Bird Johnson, Former First Lady of the United States

YOUR CHILD IS NOT A MISTAKE OR A MISHAP even if you did not plan for him or her. God has been expecting that child. The moment they were formed in you, God was there, smiling. Believe it or not that child is custom-made from God himself and has been entrusted to you with tremendous gifts to offer. You have been trusted with something valuable and you must show that you are worthy of that trust. How well are you going to care for what has been entrusted to you? That child is here for a reason. Even before they were born God knew them (Isa 44:2) Just as you cannot look at a caterpillar and predict a butterfly so also you cannot decide or predict who you think your kids are just based on the circumstances or situations they are in at the moment, you have to have faith enough that God is able to raise them through you. You also have to have faith in their abilities. Having faith in your kids sometimes may involve looking past the facts to the <u>truth</u> of who God says they are. Any feelings of inadequacy (which may be as a result of a lack of faith in themselves) your kids harbor about themselves to deliver what is expected of them, would reflect in the results they produce in every area of their lives. In order to encourage our children to reach their utmost capability we have to have faith in them before they ever prove themselves. Therefore it is imperative that as a parent you have faith in the abilities of your children, encourage them in their unique skills and talents. The faith you have in your child allows them to imbibe a self-assurance in themselves that leads to self-realization which generates further success. Usually when a child senses disapproval or contempt from their parents it mars their outlook on life and how they perceive themselves. This may even cause the child to rebel especially in their teen years (unless you can prove to them that any discipline stems from a place of loving kindness). However, your children were not born with any rebellious habits. They usually acquire these habits as they grow and just as they learned these habits they can also unlearn them.

Your kids want to hear repeatedly how much you adore and believe in them (even something as little as fondly calling them a nickname can cause them to be more receptive of your message, it can be the difference between their listening to you in order to understand your apprehensions or listening to react) and when they repeatedly receive encouragement from their parents they tend to think well of themselves and this will reflect in their behaviour and in their speech.

How parents interact with their kids such as how quickly you respond to their cries or how gruffly or gently you hold them in your arms from infancy communicates how valuable you think they are which in turn decides how they develop in the society either feeling inferior or as well mannered humans. Your belief in your child will decide a lot about them as you are about one of the first role models they will encounter in life. Managing your kids should be a priority. When your kids realize that you believe in them and that they are a priority to you it eliminates and heals any inferior feelings. It also allows them to let go of whatever feelings of inadequacy they may be harboring about themselves and encourages self esteem and self achievement.

I LIKE MYSELF NOW

"A teacher asked his student why he thought his grades had improved compared to the year before, the student replied and said because I like myself now that I am with you".

When self-doubt doesn't plague your children then their attitude will reflect that possibility and they will begin to blossom. Keep expressing your belief in them and encouraging your children daily in order to preserve them (Heb 3:13). The poem below illustrates the importance of cherishing your children today.

THE LAST TIME

From the moment you hold your baby in your arms
You will never be the same.
You might long for the person you were before,
When you had freedom and time.

And nothing in particular to worry about.

You will know tiredness like you never knew
it before,

And days will run into days that are
exactly the same,

Full of feeding and burping,

 Nappy changes and crying,

Whining and crying,

Naps or a lack of naps,

It might seem like a never ending cycle.

But don't forget…

There is a last time for everything.

There will come a time when you will feed
your baby for the very last time.

They will fall asleep on you after a long day.

And it will be the last time you ever hold
your sleeping child.

One day you will carry them on your hip,
then set them down.

And never pick them up that way again.

You will scrub their hair in the bath one night

And from that day on they will want to bath alone.

They will hold your hand to cross the road and never reach for it again.

They will creep into your room at midnight for cuddles,

And it will be the last time they ever wake to this.

One afternoon you will sing the wheels on the bus and do all the actions,

Then never sing them that song again.

They will kiss you goodbye at the gate,

The next day they will ask to walk to the gate alone.

You will read a bedtime story and wipe your last dirty face.

They will one day run to you with arms raised.

For the very last time.

The thing is you won't even know it's the last time.

Until there are no more times and even then it will take you a while to realise.

So while you are living in these times,

Remember there are only so many of them and

When they are gone,

You will yearn for just one more day of them.

For one last time.

(Author unknown)

Chapter Two

AFFIRM THE KIDS

"It is easier to build strong children than to repair broken men." — *Frederick Douglass, abolitionist and statesman*

A STUDY CONDUCTED BY THE TREMEN-dously sober and scientific Harvard University found that patients who were prayed for recovered quicker than those who weren't prayed for even if they were not aware of the prayer. For you shall decree and it shall be established. What have you decreed, that you want established? For there to be an establishment there should already be a decree in place. What are you saying about your kids? The most powerful story in the world is the story you tell yourself. What story are you telling yourself about your kids? Are you affirming and validating them or are you speaking derogatory words to them. Your ability to communicate properly with your child is also linked to your financial success because according to the Carnegie Institute of Technology, only 15% of your income is based on your technical skills. While 85% of your financial success is due to your personality and ability to communicate, negotiate, and lead. You want to lead in the workplace? Start at home.

AM I OK?

Everyone wants to be validated- someone once asked Oprah after having conducted over 37,000 interviews of the most successful people from world leaders to famous celebrities to billionaire ceos: was there any commonality between them or a common trait of success. Oprah said she noticed that after every interview the person would lean in and ask was that ok? Or did you like it? She said Barack Obama asked it, George Bush asked it and even Beyoncé asked it after she gave Oprah a dance lesson. Even the most successful people worry about being liked.

There is a psychological concept called the mirror exposure effect or the familiarity effect where researchers found that people tend to like things and people they had seen more often. The more a person is exposed to something the more they tend to like it. The more often someone sees you the more they tend to like you- so this <u>means</u> showing up for their school games, and events and the more your children see you the more they will like you and feel validated by you.

Some phrases to use when affirming your child include "I was just thinking of you" or "You are so interesting". Every time you affirm your child you are meeting their need to be understood and validated. This need to be understood, affirmed, validated and appreciated is a psychological survival need and is considered next to Physical survival.

Aim to empathically listen-listening with intent to understand - see the world the way they see it. The essence of empathic listening is not that you agree with them but that you understand them emotionally as well as intellectually or that you genuinely seek to understand them, you listen with your ears, eyes and heart for feeling, meaning and behaviour for nuance. You sense, intuit and feel. When you listen with empathy you give your children psychological air, then you can focus on problem solving or influencing them.

Most children will become what adults tell them they will become. It is very necessary that you encourage and speak life to your kids. They get enough negativity from the newspapers and other forms of media. As you communicate with them daily are you tearing them down or calling forth potential? The more you call your child 'rowdy' or 'lazy' or make cold pricklies comments such as 'good thing you are pretty because you are not too smart' the more they will behave accordingly. Self-fulfilling prophecy?

Parents and guardians have to tutor their children on the power of choice as well as the importance of affirming themselves so if for instance someone calls them an undesirable name (eg 'you are just daft) they can counter it by affirming themselves and saying what God says about them such as 'I am daily growing in wisdom and stature'. Children can also learn to replace any negative self talk such as 'I am not good enough' or "I can't accomplish anything" to affirmations such as 'I can learn anything I want to' 'I can do all things through Christ'.

This is not to say constructive criticism or negative feedback is out of place. Feedback should be specific to behaviour not the general worth of the child: Instead of saying 'you are a lazy child' you could say 'it's lazy to not prepare for your exams'. Instead of speaking belittling words, speak uplifting words such as 'you are more than a conqueror', 'you are an overcomer' and 'you have what it takes to succeed'. Never forget that mighty oaks from little acorns grow. Uplifting and encouraging verbal and nonverbal communication increases the chances of your child cooperating with you. Your duty as a parent is to call forth things that are not as though they were in your kids.

WHAT YOU ARE IS AS IMPORTANT AS WHAT YOU DO

It was a sunny Saturday afternoon in Oklahoma City. My friend and proud father

Bobby Lewis was taking his two little boys to play miniature golf. He walked up to the fellow at the ticket counter and said, "How much is it to get in?"

The young man replied, "$3.00 for you and $3.00 for any kid who is older than six. We let them in free if they are six or younger. How old are they?" Bobby replied, "The lawyer's three and the doctor is seven, so I guess I owe you $6.00."

The man at the ticket counter said, "Hey, Mister, did you just win the lottery or something? You could have saved yourself three bucks. You could have told me that the older one was six; I wouldn't have known the difference." Bobby replied, "Yes, that may be true, but the kids would have known the difference."

As Ralph Waldo Emerson said, "Who you are speaks so loudly I can't hear what you're saying." In challenging times when ethics are more important than ever before, make sure you set a good example for everyone you work and live with.

Patricia Fripp (Presentation Skills Expert)

Chapter Three

Visualize

"*Children are great imitators so give them something great to imitate*" — (anonymous)

TO VISUALIZE IS TO FORM A MENTAL VISUAL image of something or someone. What image do you have of life? What image do you have of yourself? Do you see yourself as a steward who has been entrusted to nurture that child?

The image you have of your life influences your choices; how you invest your time or utilise your talents or the principles you imbibe in your relationships with your children. The art of visualization involves imagining that you have already gotten desired results. Executives of corporations, elite athletes, celebrities and business tycoons have utilised visualization and you can utilise them too.

VISUALISATION BRINGS AN OLYMPIC GOLD MEDAL

Athletes have used visualization techniques since the 1960's. In preparing for the 1984 Olympics Peter Vidmar and Tim Daggett visualized their way to the gold medal. Every day after the coaches and everyone had left Peter Vidmar and Tim Daggett would practice some more at the University of California, Los Angeles (UCLA) gym and round off their workouts visualizing they were at the Olympics and getting the perfect score and receiving the gold medal, they kept visualizing that every day for four years until the Olympics. At the Olympics they carried on their routine as they had pictured themselves at the UCLA gym and just carried out their routine like they were at a UCLA practice and guess what they won the gold medal.

Tim Daggett

Owner, Daggett Gymnastics - NBC Sports Color Analyst - Motivational Speaker

When visualizing, some recommend a vision board which is a group of images you look at to realise a certain outcome.

You may also decide to set aside a few minutes each day preferably when you just wake up in the morning, close your eyes and see yourself connecting with your kids, see yourself overcoming any barriers and getting along with them.

Visualization activates your creative subconscious which will generate creative propositions to help you achieve your goals- (which in this case are responsible kids).

THROW YOUR HEART OVER THE BAR

A famous trapeze artist was instructing his students how to perform on the high trapeze bar. Finally, having given full explanations in this skill, he told them to demonstrate their ability. One student, looking up at the insecure perch upon which he must perform, was suddenly filled with fear. He froze completely. He had a terrifying vision of himself falling to the ground. He couldn't move a muscle, so deep was his fright. "I can't do it!"

He gasped. The instructor put his arm around the boy's shoulder and said, "Son, you can do it, and I will tell you how." Then he made one of the wisest remarks I have ever heard. He said, "Throw your heart over the bar and your body will follow."

Visualization programs your brain to readily perceive and recognize the resources you need to achieve your dreams.

Visualization activates the law of attraction, drawing into your life the persons, resources and circumstances you need to achieve your goals.

Visualization builds your internal motivation to take steps that are necessary to achieve your aspirations and goals. As parents we practice visualization as regards our dreams- imagining them as already accomplished, now visualize your kids as already having achieved their goals, visualise them as having learnt that new sport they have been training to learn. Visualise your kid as the highest goal scorer, the valedictorian or the prom queen or teen Miss Usa because as far as you see so will God give unto you. (Gen 13: 14-17).

You can also teach your children visualization. They can spend five minutes a day visualizing their goals and objectives as already accomplished. They can have a clear vision of their goals as if they had already achieved them. This would motivate the children, enhance their creativity and help them form perceptions of their environment and themselves.

Chapter Four

Expect results

"Faith is to believe what you do not see; the reward of this faith is to see what you believe." — *Saint Augustine*

As you commence on this voyage into Positive Discipline, it is essential to have a destination in mind, and a compass to help you get there. Having a catalog of attributes and life skills you hope to have your children develop, can serve as your compass.

According to William James 'Our belief at the beginning of a doubtful undertaking is the one thing that ensures a successful outcome'. Choose to believe that what you want is possible.

Your mind is so powerful that it will manifest whatever you want through positive expectations. Scientists were of the notion that human beings responded to information flowing into the brain from the outside world, however, in recent times scientists now believe we respond based on what the brain expects to happen (based on past experiences).

A metaphysician once said, "If you do not run your subconscious mind yourself, someone else will run it for you." Parents sometimes, unknowingly, draw ill situations to their children, by continuously harboring fearful thoughts. For example: A friend asked a woman if her child had the flu. Her response was "not yet!" As if she was expecting the flu or preparing for it.

NOTHING WRONG.

According to one physician, "Many of my patients have nothing wrong with them except their thoughts. So I write them a prescription. It is a verse from the Bible, Romans 12:2. I make them look it up. The verse reads: "Do not be conformed to this world, but be transformed by the renewing of your mind."

THE HIGHEST SCORE.

A young boy went with his mother to his faith teacher asking that she "speak the word" for his imminent examinations. He was given this affirmation "I am one with Infinite Intelligence. I know everything I should know on this subject." He had excellent knowledge of other subjects, but not arithmetic. She met him afterwards, and he said: "I spoke the word for my arithmetic, and scored the highest score;

When you expect nothing but the best for your children you release a magnetic force that draws only the best. As God guides your mind, that which seemingly was impossible becomes possible.

Develop your faith power by saturating your minds with God's word, if you can, spend at least an hour studying and retaining God's word in your memory by saying them over and over (the Scriptures are read by more people than any other book and humanity has more confidence in it than any other document written). If you can believe, all things are possible to him that believes (Mark 9:23). In the process of studying God's word you will be transformed and your expectations will increase. You can achieve even the most unbelievable things by faith power. As you affirm your children daily and speak life which is in the power of your tongue (Prov 18:21) over your children, expect astonishing results.

Chapter Five

Scriptures and Confessions

(ALL SCRIPTURES FROM THE BEREAN STUDY BIBLE)

THE STATEMENT THAT THE BIBLE IS GOD'S word is a confession of faith, a statement of the faith which hears God Himself speak through the biblical word of man.

-Karl Barth in Alan G. Padgett, Steve Wilkens Christianity and Western Thought, Volume 3:

Journey to Postmodernity in the Twentieth Century

Andrei Bitov, a Russian novelist, grew up under an atheistic Communist regime. But God got his attention one dreary day. He recalls, "In my twenty-seventh year, while riding the metro in Leningrad (now St. Petersburg) I was overcome with a despair so great that life seemed to stop at once, pre-empting the future entirely, let alone any meaning. Suddenly, all by itself, a phrase appeared: Without God life makes no sense. Repeating it in astonishment, I rode the phrase up like a moving staircase, got out of the metro and walked into God's light." You may have felt in the dark about your child's purpose in life. Congratulations, you're about to walk into the light.

Deuteronomy 28:13

Scripture: The LORD will make you the head and not the tail; you will only move upward and never downward, if you hear and carefully follow the commandments of the LORD your God, which I am giving you today.

Confession- You are the head and not the tail above and not beneath.

Deuteronomy 30:6

Scripture: The LORD your God will circumcise your hearts and the hearts of your descendants, and you will love Him with all your heart and with all your soul, so that you may live.

Confession: You have a circumcised heart and you love the lord your God.

Deuteronomy 33:25

..May the bolts of your gate be iron and bronze, and may your strength match your days."

Confession: As your days are so shall your strength be.

Numbers 6:24

Scripture: May the LORD bless you and keep you;

Confession: You are blessed of the lord.

Nehemiah 8:10

Scripture: Then Nehemiah told them, "Go and eat what is rich, drink what is sweet, and send out portions to those who have nothing prepared, since today is holy to our Lord. Do not grieve, for the joy of the LORD is your strength."

Confession: The joy of the lord is your strength.

Isaiah 40:31

Scripture: But those who wait upon the LORD will renew their strength; they will mount up with wings like eagles; they will run and not grow weary, they will walk and not faint.

Confession: You will mount up with wings like the eagle.

Isaiah 41:10

Scripture: Do not fear, for I am with you; do not be afraid, for I am your God. I will strengthen you; I will surely help you; I will uphold you with My right hand of righteousness.

Confession: You are strong in the lord.

Isaiah 50:4

Scripture: The Lord GOD has given Me the tongue of discipleship, to sustain the weary with a word. He awakens Me morning by morning; He awakens My ear to listen as a disciple.

Confession: You have the tongue of
the learned.

Isaiah 54:13

Then all your sons will be taught by the
LORD, and great will be their prosperity.

Confession: You are taught of God and you
are prosperous

Isaiah 54:14

In righteousness you will be established, far
from oppression, for you will have no fear.

Terror will be far removed, for it will not
come near you.

Confession: You are established in righteousness and far from oppression, there is no fear in you and terror is removed from you.

Isaiah 54:17

Scripture: No weapon formed against you shall prosper, and you will refute every tongue that accuses you. This is the heritage of the servants of the LORD, and their vindication is from Me," declares the LORD.

Confession: No weapon formed against you will prosper.

Psalm 103:5

Scripture: who satisfies you with good things, so that your youth is renewed like the eagle's.

Confession: Your youth is renewed like the eagle.

Psalm 103:5

who satisfies you with good things, so that your youth is renewed like the eagle's.

Confession: God is filling your life with blessings and you are becoming younger and younger each day.

Psalm 118:24

Scripture: This is the day that the LORD has made; we will rejoice and be glad in it

Confession: You will rejoice in this day.

Psalm 119:11

Scripture: I have hidden Your word in my heart that I might not sin against You.

Confession: You have hidden God's word in your heart so that you would not sin against him.

Psalm 119:105

Scripture: Your word is a lamp to my feet and a light to my path.

Confession: God's word is a lamp unto your feet and a light for my path.

Psalm 5:12

Scripture: For surely You, O LORD, bless the righteous; You surround them with the shield of Your favor.

Confession: God's favor is around you like a shield.

Psalm 101:2

Scripture: I will ponder the way that is blameless—when will You come to me? I will walk in my house with integrity of heart.

Confession: You will behave yourself wisely in a perfect way.

Psalm 101:4

Scripture: A perverse heart shall depart from me; I will know nothing of evil.

Confession: You will not know a wicked person.

Psalm 107:2

Scripture: Let the redeemed of the LORD say so, whom He has redeemed from the hand of the enemy.

Confession: You are redeemed of the lord.

Psalm 127:3

Scripture "Children are indeed a heritage from the lord and the fruit of the womb his reward.

Confession: You are a reward from God

Psalm 139:13-14

Scripture: For You formed my inmost being; You knit me together in my mother's womb. I praise You, for I am fearfully and wonderfully made. Marvelous are Your works, and I know this very well.

Confession: You are fearfully and wonderfully made.

Proverbs 25:28

Scripture: Like a city whose walls are broken down is a man who does not control his temper.

Confession: You have self-control

Proverbs 1; 8-9

Listen my son to your father's instruction and do not forsake the teaching of your mother. For they are a garland of grace on your head and a pendant around your neck.

Confession: You are attentive to your parent's instructions.

Proverbs 28:1
Scripture: The wicked flee when no one pursues, but the righteous are as bold as a lion.

Confession: You are as bold as a lion.

Luke 2:52
Scripture: And Jesus grew in wisdom and stature, and in favor with God and man.

Confession: You are growing in wisdom and stature in favor with God and Man.

Philippians 4:8

Scripture: Finally, brothers, whatever is true, whatever is honorable, whatever is right, whatever is pure, whatever is lovely, whatever is admirable—if anything is excellent or praiseworthy—think on these things

Confession: You focus on what is true, honorable, right, pure, lovely and admirable and you only dwell on what is excellent and worthy of praise.

Phillipians 4:13

Scripture: I can do all things through Christ who gives me strength.

Confession: You can do all through Christ's strength.

1st Corinthians 2:16

Scripture: For who has known the mind of the Lord, so as to instruct Him?" But we have the mind of Christ.

Confession: You have the mind of Christ

1st Corinthians 6:19

Scripture: Do you not know that your body is a temple of the Holy Spirit who is in you, whom you have received from God? You are not your own.

Confession: My body is the dwelling place of the Holy Spirit

2nd Corinthians 5:17

Scripture: Therefore if anyone is in Christ, he is a new creation. The old has passed away. Behold, the new has come.

Confession: You are a new creation in Christ.

Colossians 2:10

Scripture: And you have been made complete in Christ, who is the head over every ruler and authority.

Confession: You are complete in him

2nd Timothy 1:7

Scripture: For God has not given us a spirit of fear, but of power, love, and self-control.

Confession: God has given you a Spirit of power, love and a sound mind.

Titus 2: 11-12

Scripture: For the grace of God has appeared, bringing salvation to everyone. It instructs us to renounce ungodliness and worldly passions, and to live sensible upright and godly lives in the present age, as we await the blessed hope and glorious appearance of our great God and saviour Jesus Christ.

Confession: You live an upright and godly life.

1st Peter 1:8

Scripture: Though you have not seen Him, you love Him; and though you do not see Him now, you believe in Him and rejoice with an inexpressible and glorious joy

Confession: You have joy unspeakable.

John 10:3

Scripture: The gatekeeper opens the gate for him, and the sheep listens for his voice. He calls his own sheep by name and leads them out.

Confession: You are Jesus little sheep and you will not follow the voice of strangers.

1st John 4:4

Scripture: You, little children, are from God and have overcome them, because greater is He who is in you than he who is in the world.

Confession: The greater one is in you.

Ephesians 3:20

Scripture: Children obey your parents in everything for this is pleasing to the lord.

Confession: You are obedient to authority

Ephesians 6:2

Scripture: "Honor your father and mother" (which is the first commandment with a promise)

Confession: You obey your parents and you have a long life.

Romans 8:37

Scripture: No, in all these things we are more than conquerors through Him who loved us.

Confession: You are more than a conqueror.

Do you know the lord?

Therefore if anyone is in
Christ, he is a new creation.
The old has passed away.
Behold, the new has come!
2nd Corinthians 5: 17

Vote King Jesus in your life by asking him to
reign in your life today.

If this book has been a blessing I would like
for you to send your stories and testimonials
to impelnow.com

Acknowledgements

Many thanks to all who made this book a success.

9 781662 800924